Rio de Janeiro's locals call their the Marvelous City. If that sounds a here – you'll soon see it isn't an id. stages. First, I was seduced by the natural features: wide, golden beaches, dramatic mountains and a huge forest hiding waterfalls and wildlife. Then, it was the city's culture that got me: buzzing samba clubs, colorful street art, busy markets full of tropical fruits bursting with flavor, and, of course, the music – samba, bossa nova, forro, baile funk – all of which combine to create a celebratory soundtrack for the city.

Underpinning Rio's natural and cultural riches are its people, known as Cariocas. They are warm, generous, and quick to laugh, sing and dance – even for a mildly grumpy gringo like me, the Carioca passion for life is contagious. While crime can be an issue, reports of Rio's security problems are often exaggerated. Still, some parts of the city should be approached with caution or only with a guide. My own knowledge of this vibrant city has been deeply enriched over the years through being married to a local; that is probably a step too far for most of you, so use this guide instead as a way to connect with the very best of Rio de Janeiro.

the hunt rio de janeiro writer

tom le mesurier

In 2009, Tom Le Mesurier left London looking for adventure. He spent the next year traveling through South and Central America until a chance meeting with a Brazilian journalist in Nicaragua led him to Rio de Janeiro. He fell in love with the journalist and her city; four short months later they were married, and Tom was learning Portuguese. Today, Tom lives in Santa Teresa and takes guests on culinary walking tours while sharing restaurant recommendations on his website, eatrio.net. When it comes to finding new bars and restaurants, Tom likes to think of himself as a dedicated researcher, but really, he's just greedy.

where to lay
your weary head

Rest up, relax and recharge

CASA BELEZA

CASA BELEZA

Lovely bed and breakfast

Rua Laurinda Santos Lobo, 311 (near Rua Monte Alegre)
+55 21 2224 7403 / casabeleza.com

Double from R$290

Set in the very heart of Santa Teresa, Casa Beleza is like something out of *The Secret Garden*. The 1930s mansion is surrounded by a walled lawn, which leads to the pool, then out to the property's expansive 1,700 sq m (18,300 sq ft) of forest. There are three spacious and individually decorated rooms in one wing of the house, and two separate apartments with private terraces set in the gardens. Owner Bindu and her delightful family live on site and will make you feel completely relaxed, while the tranquil ambiance will have you feeling a million miles from the hustle and bustle of the Zona Sul neighborhoods, even though they're only 20 minutes away.

CASA MOSQUITO

Romantic getaway

Rua Saint Roman, 222 (near Rua Piragibe Frota Águiar)
+55 21 3586 5042 / casamosquito.com

Double from R$800

This chic hotel is located in the hills where Ipanema
and Copacabana meet. There are some steep steps leading from
the gate to the hotel, but the climb feels oh so worth it when you
see this light, airy space full of stylish touches and eclectic design.
French owners Benjamin and Louis have somehow managed
to create a space that feels simultaneously luxe and laid-back.
With its beautiful terraces hung with hammocks and a spectacular
rooftop infinity pool, you may find yourself reluctant to leave.

LA SUITE

Luxurious style

Rua Jackson de Figueiredo, 501 (near Estrada do Joá)
+55 21 3259 6123 / bydussol.com/la-suite

Double from R$900

La Suite, located in the exclusive neighborhood of Joá, is pretty
much the definition of a high-end boutique hotel. Owned by two
brothers from France, the property consists of seven sumptuous
rooms individually themed by color and punctuated by antiques,
period furniture and art. But there are more reasons to stay here
than the design: the staff is incredibly helpful, there's a rooftop
pool, and, perhaps most magnificent of all, the hotel almost hangs
over the sea – the views will leave you gasping.

MARTA'S RIO DE JANEIRO GUESTHOUSE

Experience beachfront living

Rua Francisco Sá, 5 (near Avenida Atlântica)
+55 21 2521 8568 / martarioguesthouse.com

Double from R$380

Occupying the top two floors of a 12-story oceanfront building in Copacabana is this terrific guesthouse. It's perfect for beach lovers looking for a home away from home, and wanting to avoid the overpriced business hotels so common in tourist areas (you know, the kind where everything is beige). The six rooms feel homey, and the view from the large terrace is pure gold. This part of Copacabana is a short walk from Ipanema, meaning that you're within 10 minutes of enjoying the bars, restaurants and beach along the whole stretch. Owner Marta Miller is friendly, speaks fluent English and is always delighted to help guests with advice and recommendations for activities and nearby restaurants.

QUINTA AZUL

Tropical chic digs

Rua Almirante Alexandrino, 256 (near Rua Santa Cristina)
+55 21 3253 1021 / quintaazul.com

Double from R$440

This swanky guesthouse is a few minutes' walk from the Santa Teresa tram stop at Largo do Curvelo, as well as many of the neighborhood's bars and restaurants such as Armazem São Thiago (see pg 13) and Bar do Mineiro (see pg 96). There are 13 rooms with varying levels of posh amenities – the deluxe rooms, for example, include large terraces with hot tubs – but all have air-conditioning, flat screen TVs and beds made with comfortable, high thread count sheets. The garden is full of trees, so don't be surprised if a few monkeys join you for the complimentary breakfast on the terrace.

RIO PANORAMIC

Art Deco mansion with breathtaking vistas

Rua Ladeira do Meireles, 196 (near Rua Almirante Alexandrino)
+55 21 3489 5196 / riopanoramichotel.com

Double from R$490

Even by this city's very high standards, the views from Rio Panoramic are stunning, and the hotel is aptly named. This marvelous B&B at the top of Santa Teresa has three massive rooms, which have been lovingly restored to include huge beds, elegant, tiled bathrooms and art from the Spanish owner's personal collection displayed on the walls. The house has high ceilings throughout, spacious lounges, and a garden with a huge sun terrace, a pool and 270-degree views across Guanabara Bay and Sugarloaf Mountain. Yes, please.

RIO PANORAMIC

santa teresa

catete, flamengo, laranjeiras

Perhaps it's wrong to have favorites, but I can't help myself: Santa Teresa, known to many as simply "Santa", is the neighborhood I call home, and after more than five years, I still find the steep hills, cobbled streets, ancient bars and small guesthouses utterly charming. Plus, the jaw-dropping views across the city definitely don't hurt. It's difficult to find a description of this area that doesn't use the word "bohemian" and there's a reason for that: located right outside of the downtown financial district, this is the creative heart of the city, a hilltop enclave that has always attracted poets, artists and dreamers. On the south side of the hill, nearby neighborhoods Catete, Flamengo and Laranjeiras share Santa's vibe and have very business-friendly rent prices; thus, inventive entrepreneurs have moved here, opening up phenomenal pizza joints and funky bars.

1 Alda Maria Doces Portugueses
2 Armazém São Thiago
3 Botero
4 Ferro e Farinha
5 Gamar Brinquedos
6 La Vereda
7 Maracatu Brasil
8 Paris Bar
9 Tacacá do Norte
10 Tucum

ALDA MARIA DOCES PORTUGUESES

Sweet family-run pastry shop

Rua Almirante Alexandrino, 1116 (near Rua Áurea) / +55 21 2232 1320
aldamaria.com.br / Closed Monday

One of Santa Teresa's treasures, this enchanting old house covered in captivating blue and white Portuguese tiles is home to Alda Maria and her bakery. Using organic sugar, free-range eggs and recipes handed down from Alda's grandmother, the whole family helps prepare Portuguese sweets and pastries, including the fabulous pastel de nata (egg tart). In addition to using their house as a café, the family has also converted one corner of their living room into a museum where you can see the original baking equipment and old photos from the family's past seven generations of bakers.

ARMAZÉM SÃO THIAGO

The quintessential Santa Teresa bar

Rua Áurea, 26 (near Rua Monte Alegre) / +55 21 2232 0822
armazemsaothiago.com.br / Open daily

Better known by its nickname, Bar do Gomez (in honor of a much-loved barman), Armazém São Thiago is my go-to local. Founded in 1919 by a Spanish immigrant and owned by his grandson today, this superb old pub epitomizes the area's allure. The pretty interior features a marble bar, dark wood paneling and walls covered in old family photos and bottles of cachaça, the national spirit. In addition to the obligatory ice-cold beer, order the bolinhos mistos, tasty bean croquettes stuffed with cured beef. On sunny days, the lively mix of clients spills outside to enjoy their drinks in the open air.

BOTERO

Brazilian comfort food

**Rua das Laranjeiras, 90 (near Rua Gago Coutinho) / +55 21 3235 6314
facebook.com/BoteroBar / Closed Monday**

Chef and co-owner Bruno Magalhães worked at several acclaimed
restaurants (including Public in New York) before returning home to Rio
to open Botero in 2012. The bar is located in an old market that surrounds
a semi-open courtyard paved in rough stone and scattered with plants.
The informal surrounds blend seamlessly with an inventive and varied
menu full of appetizing local standards, which are a great size for sharing.
This spot attracts a friendly crowd and things usually get quite busy
on weekends. On Saturdays, Botero serves up an excellent feijoada, a
traditional stew of black beans, beef and pork, and often has live samba
performances as well.

FERRO E FARINHA

Exquisite pizza with New York roots

Rua Andrade Pertence, 42 (near Rua do Catete) / No phone
facebook.com/FerroEFarinha / Closed Monday and Tuesday

A few years ago, Sei Shiroma quit an unfulfilling advertising job in New York, learned to make Neapolitan-style pizzas and moved to Rio. When I met him, Sei was using a custom-made oven on the back of a trailer to sell pizzas on the city streets under the name Ferro e Farinha ("Iron & Flour"). In a town notorious for bad pizza, Sei's flavorful creations, featuring toppings such as spiced honey, garlic confit and miso, soon won him quite a following, so in 2014 he traded the trailer for this snug yet modish restaurant. Today the secret is out, so arrive early and expect to wait for your pie – it'll be worth it.

GAMAR BRINQUEDOS

Classical toys

Rua Almirante Alexandrino, 470 (near Rua Carlos Brant)
+55 21 99339 3993 / magoobrinquedos.com.br / Open daily

Call me a grumpy old man, but when it comes to buying presents for kids,
I really can't stand those battery-powered, plastic monstrosities that play
incessant music. You can imagine my delight, then, when I discovered
Gamar Brinquedos, a store selling clever wooden toys and games that
encourage children to actively play rather than sit back as spectators.
The store's ancient stone walls are lined with display shelves and cabinets
full of well-constructed puzzles, kaleidoscopes and whole menageries
of wooden animals, clowns and fantastical dragons. The best part?
There's not a flashing light or "batteries not included" label in sight!

LA VEREDA

Tasteful gifts

Rua Almirante Alexandrino, 428 (near Rua Carlos Brant)
+55 21 2507 0317 / lavereda.art.br / Open daily

While Santa Teresa has more than its fair share of independent stores, cozy guesthouses and endearing bars, when it comes to souvenir shopping, you'll have to look carefully if you want to avoid tacky T-shirts. La Vereda is where I go when I'm looking for something unique. Located in the heart of the neighborhood, this pretty shop is crammed from floor to ceiling with desirable handmade items ranging from prints, paintings and ceramics to hammocks, clothes and jewelry.

MARACATU BRASIL

Brazilian percussion lessons

Rua Ipiranga, 49 (near Rua Conde de Baependi) / **+55 21 2557 4754**
maracatubrasil.com.br / **Closed Sunday**

While a trip to the movies or theater in Rio is going to yield limited returns for non-Portuguese speakers, music is one of those great pleasures that transcends the limitations of language. Brazil is home to a wealth of percussion styles and rhythms – many with indigenous and African roots. Maracatu Brasil in Laranjeiras not only sells new and used drums, shakers and a variety of other percussive noisemakers, but also hosts lessons and exhibitions from local teachers and performers for both children and adults. Here, you can learn Brazilian percussion instruments like the cuíca and tambor, as well as styles like samba and batuque.

PARIS BAR

Masterful cocktails in grand surrounds

Praia do Flamengo, 340 (near Rua Cruz Lima) / +55 21 2551 1278
parisbar.com.br / Closed Sunday and Monday

Paris Bar takes its drinks very seriously – no piña coladas with umbrellas on
top here. The star of the show is Alex Mesquita, a barman who has won so
many awards for his mixology skills that he must have a dedicated trophy
room. Set in the splendiferous Casa Julieta de Serpa in Flamengo, the décor
is all marble staircases and crystal chandeliers, and the food is mostly
fancy bar snacks – carpaccios and bruschettas – but the drinks are what
this place is all about. On a recent visit, I tried the spectacular Al Capone, a
blend of Japanese whisky and Angostura bitters that was served wreathed
in fragrant smoke. Expect premium ingredients, hand-carved ice, cutting-
edge techniques and a steep bill!

TACACÁ DO NORTE

Amazonian cuisine for adventurous diners

Rua Barão do Flamengo, 35 (Rua Senador Vergueriro)
+55 21 2205 7545 / No website / Open daily

When guests on my food tours describe themselves as culinarily daring,
I take them directly to Tacacá do Norte. This no-frills restaurant specializes
in fare from Pará, a large state in northern Brazil, which covers a huge area of
the Amazon. The establishment is named after tacacá, an extraordinary soup
that includes jambú, an herb that leaves your mouth tingling and numb.
Other highlights are the puréed açaí berry slushie topped with crunchy
tapioca pieces and an amazing selection of juices and ice creams made from
obscure fruits such as bacurí and cupuaçu that rarely make it out of the
Amazon. Though it's not for the faint of heart, it does draw a crowd;
if you want to avoid the masses, visit on a weekday, when it's less busy.

TUCUM

Indigenous handicrafts

Rua Paschoal Carlos Magno, 100 (near Rua Felício dos Santos)
+55 21 3128 2957 / loja.tucumbrasil.com / Closed Sunday and Monday

Founded in 2013 by Amanda Santana and her anthropologist husband Fernando as a way to support some of Brazil's 200-plus tribes and bring their goods to a wider market, Tucum is a homey store crammed full of remarkable handmade goods. Sadly, many native communities are exploited by unscrupulous resellers, but, in contrast, Tucum has strong links with over 40 villages, paying them fair prices and supporting their struggle for rights and, in some cases, even existence. Highlights include bracelets, earrings and necklaces featuring intricate beadwork, handbags and colorful woven baskets that can be used as planters or a decorative way to tidy up your house.

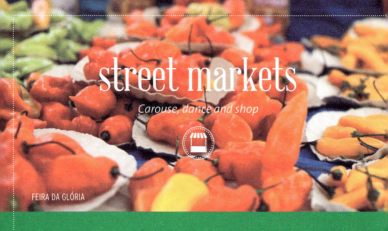

street markets

Carouse, dance and shop

FEIRA DA GLÓRIA

Exploring Rio's outstanding feiras de rua (street markets) is an activity I love: browsing the fresh produce, eyeballing antiques, ogling the shellfish and tasting everything that looks good. But markets here aren't just about selling – they also include live music, street performers, dancing and street food stalls. Be sure to watch your belongings, and always ask for permission before snapping photos.

Though it's open daily, **Feira de São Cristóvão** really comes alive on weekends, and combines cultural aspects of Northeastern Brazil, from live forró music to dozens of restaurants serving classics such as cabrito ensopado (goat stew) and queijo coalho (northeastern cheese, grilled and served with molasses). Don't expect vendors to speak English, but go with a smile and a spirit of adventure and you'll have a fabulous day out.

In Lapa on the first Saturday of the month? Then head to **Feira Rio Antigo** on Rua do Lavradio. This ancient street is closed to traffic and scores of street stalls are set up to sell antiques of all kinds. From furniture and lampshades to old tea sets and cutlery, there's plenty to feast your eyes on.

Every Sunday, **Feira da Glória** sets up near the Glória metro station and sells fresh, flavorful fruits. The stallholders are always friendly and will often invite you to sample their stock without any obligation to make a purchase. In the months leading up to Carnival, you may be lucky enough to spy bands practicing behind the stalls.

FEIRA DA GENERAL GLICÉRIO
Rua General Glicério (near Rua Belisário Távora)
facebook.com/feirasorganicas, open Tuesday

FEIRA DA GLÓRIA
Avenida Augusto Severo (near Rua Teixeira da
Freitas), open Sunday

FEIRA DE SÃO CRISTÓVÃO
Pavilhão de São Cristóvão
(near Campo de São Cristóvão), +55 21 2580 5335
feiradesaocristovao.org.br, closed Monday

FEIRA RIO ANTIGO
Rua do Lavradio (near Rua Visconde do Rio Branco)
+55 21 2224 6693, novorioantigo.com.br
open first Saturday of the month

PEIXARIA Z-13
Posto 6, Avenida Atlântica (near Rua Francisco
Otaviano), +55 21 2523 4151, peixariaz13.com.br
closed Sunday

Considering how much coastline there is in Rio, there are relatively few seafood restaurants. For super fresh fish, wake up early and head over to **Peixaria Z-13**, a small fish market at the Ipanema-end of the beach in Copacabana. Local fishermen haul their boats up onto the sand to deliver their catch, and you can even have someone shuck your oysters so you can enjoy them right on the beach.

Reserve a Saturday for **Feira da General Glicério** in Laranjeiras if you fancy your markets with music. There are market stalls selling a wide array of fresh produce, clothes, jewelry and street food. In the center of it all is a band playing chorinho, a melodic form of samba that can inspire a hundred or more locals to spontaneously burst into song. It gives me goosebumps every time.

botafogo

humaitá, urca

Botafogo and its residential counterpart, Humaitá, might be Rio's best kept secret. With no high-profile attractions, this area has (so far) gone unnoticed by most tourists. However, its proximity to Copacabana, handy transport links and low rent prices have made it an attractive spot in recent years for some outstanding bars, restaurants, shops and mixed-use businesses. As with New York's Brooklyn or London's Shoreditch, Botafogo is an intriguing mix of old and new. Colonial mansions and ancient restaurants sit alongside dive bars, rock clubs and experimental spaces dedicated to art, food and music. And like Urca to the east, it also happens to boast its own stretch of beach real estate. Although it hasn't quite reached peak hipster levels, I have a feeling that in five years, there will be people lamenting that they liked Botafogo before it was cool.

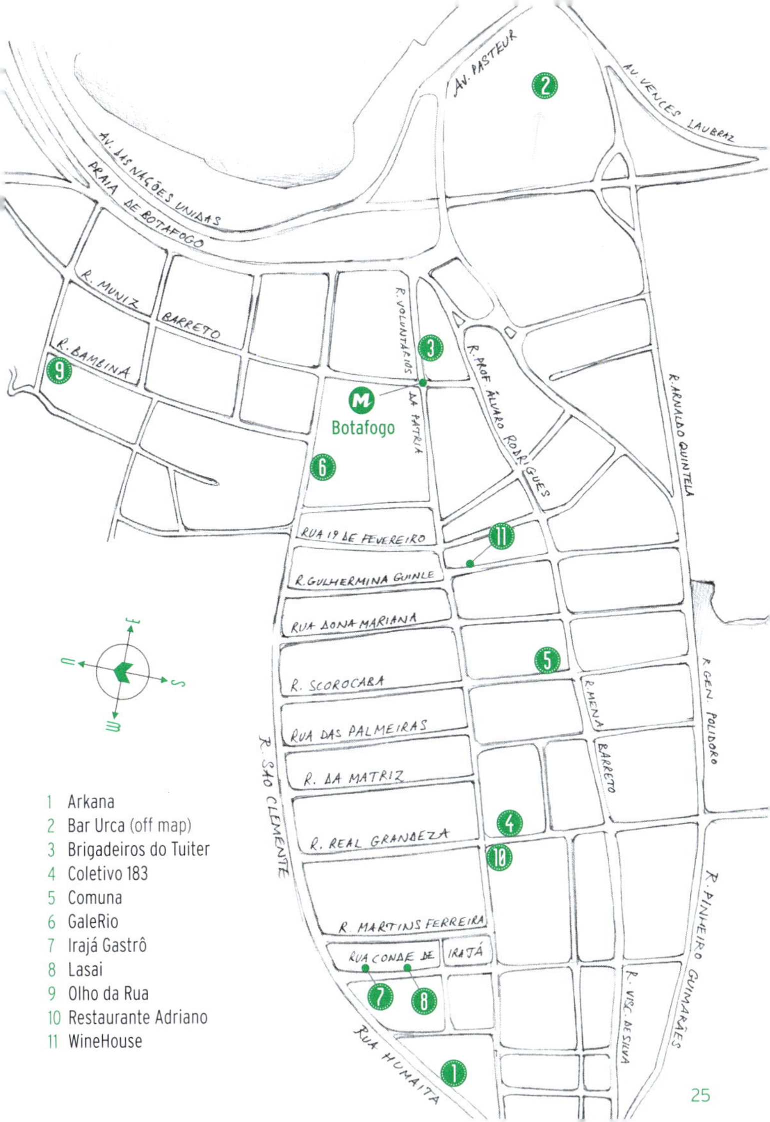
AV. PASTEUR
AV. VENCES LAUBRAZ
AV. DAS NAÇÕES UNIDAS
PRAIA DE BOTAFOGO
R. MUNIZ BARRETO
R. BAMBINA
R. VOLUNTÁRIOS DA PATRIA
Botafogo
R. PROF. ÁLVARO RODRIGUES
R. ARNALDO QUINTELA
RUA 19 DE FEVEREIRO
R. GULHERMINA GUINLE
RUA DONA MARIANA
R. SCOROCABA
R. MENA BARRETO
R. GEN. POLIDORO
RUA DAS PALMEIRAS
R. SÃO CLEMENTE
R. DA MATRIZ
R. REAL GRANDEZA
R. MARTINS FERREIRA
RUA CONDE DE IRAJÁ
R. PINHEIRO GUIMARÃES
R. VISC. DE SILVA
RUA HUMAITÁ
N
O
S
E

1 Arkana
2 Bar Urca (off map)
3 Brigadeiros do Tuiter
4 Coletivo 183
5 Comuna
6 GaleRio
7 Irajá Gastrô
8 Lasai
9 Olho da Rua
10 Restaurante Adriano
11 WineHouse

ARKANA

Rich treasure trove for gift hunters

Rua Humaitá, 63A (near Rua Voluntários da Pátria)
+55 21 2226 7187 / arkana.com.br / Open daily

I've always loved shops that need to be explored rather than merely given a once-over. Whether I'm in a bookstore or a shop selling curios, I enjoy it more if I have to dig through boxes, scan through crowded shelves or hunt through hidden back rooms. That makes Arkana my kind of place. Designer Ricardo Mourthé has assembled an amazing assortment of lampshades, prints and paintings, sculptures, toys, ornaments, clocks; the list is seemingly endless. The objects are vibrant, eclectic and novel – and the store? Completely overcrowded! To fit everything in comfortably, you'd probably need a store twice the size, but where's the fun in that? A great place if you're looking for presents.

BAR URCA

Beer and snacks with breathtaking views

Rua Cândido Gafree, 205 (at Avenida João Luís Alves)
+55 21 2295 8744 / barurca.com.br / Open daily

If I could take you to only one bar here, this would be it. Bar Urca, an unassuming hole-in-the-wall, provides one of the quintessential Rio experiences: to while away a sunny afternoon, sitting on the mureta (long, stone wall) opposite the bar, sipping something icy cold and nibbling on tasty bar bites, such as crunchy pasteis (deep-fried pastry pockets) and empadinhas (buttery, crumbly pies). Located out on the Urca peninsula in the shadow of Sugarloaf Mountain, the views across Guanabara Bay are wondrous. As the sun dips below the horizon, large crowds of locals mix with a smattering of well-informed tourists, as everyone revels in the glorious palette of colors, basking in the palpable feeling of how good it is to be alive.

BRIGADEIROS DO TUITER

A multitude of Brazil's favorite candy

Rua Voluntários da Pátria, 45, Store 108 (near Rua Nelson Mandela)
+55 21 3936 7212 / **brigadeirosdotuiter.com.br** / **Closed Sunday**

The Brazilian love of red meat is well known, but it wasn't until I got here that I discovered that they also have a very sweet tooth. I present as evidence the love, which borders on obsession, Brazilians have for brigadeiro, a truffle-sized candy made primarily of condensed milk and chocolate powder. For my taste, the original recipe is sickly sweet and needs something extra to balance out all that sugar. Apparently Palomar Cordeiro agreed: she opened this cute shop that sports a floral motif reminiscent of a Cath Kidston design, and sells over 40 different varieties of brigadeiro – far more than you'll find elsewhere – including carrot cake, Grana Padano cheese and, my newest fancy, brigadeiro brulèe.

COLETIVO 183

Indie women's fashion

Rua Real Grandeza, 183 (near Rua Henrique de Novais)
+55 21 22281 031 / facebook.com/coletivo183
Closed Saturday and Sunday

When it comes to shopping for women's clothes, the majority of Rio's stores are located within vast shopping malls, and the items for sale tend to be mass-produced. If you're looking for something unique and trendy, and you prefer the experience of browsing vintage stores and designer studios, then Coletivo 183 will be much more to your liking. Housed in the rooms of a 19th-century mansion, this boutique displays handcrafted clothes, jewelry and accessories from an independent collective of young designers. Chief among the brands is Biombo, a collection of light, summery dresses featuring daring prints and dazzling colors – terrific for hot summer evenings.

COMUNA

Bar, gallery and home of Rio's best burger

Rua Sorocaba, 585 (near Rua Mena Barreto) / +55 21 3029 0789
comuna.cc / Closed Monday

This is a marvelous example of what's making Botafogo such an exciting neighborhood right now. Instead of following conventional models, business owners are experimenting with new ideas and formats. Comuna is as close as this city gets to a hipster hangout: there's no sign above the door and although it's primarily a bar, the upstairs area functions as an art gallery, clothing store and live music venue. Contrary to what you might expect, being so multi-functional doesn't seem to have watered down the quality – the cocktails are excellent and they have won local magazine *Veja Rio*'s award for yummiest burger twice.

GALERIO

Street art galore

Rua São Clemente, 117 (near Rua Estácio Coimbra)
+55 21 2245 2007 / facebook.com/GaleRio.Oficial / Closed Saturday and Sunday

Rio's thriving graffiti scene is one of the first things visitors see when they arrive. In the past, the authorities treated all graffiti as something to be erased and eradicated, but in recent years, City Hall has started to realize that urban art can be a force for good: brightening the city and inspiring creativity in young members of the poorest communities. To reflect this thawing of attitudes, this gallery devoted purely to street art was opened in 2015 by city-run Instituto EixoRio, and features work from some of the town's most important artists, such as Marcelo Lamarca and Cazé Sawaya. What's more, admission is free.

IRAJÁ GASTRÔ

Deconstructed Brazilian cuisine

Rua Conde de Irajá, 109 (near Rua São Clemente)
+55 21 2246 1395 / irajagastro.com.br / Open daily

I'm a huge fan of Rio's local fare, but it's impossible to describe the classics as delicate – for many, the ideal postprandial activity is a three-hour snooze on the nearest sofa. To counter this, Chef Pedro Artagão deconstructs those recipes and gives them a lighter touch – for example, arroz piamontese (creamy rice, beef and gravy) becomes a cheese risotto served with a beautiful piece of filet mignon. His restaurant, Irajá Gastrô, is housed in a white-washed mansion with a modern interior, and tables spread across several different spaces including a well-lit conservatory, a narrow corridor with bar seating, a cushy lounge area and the eight-seat chef's table. Don't skip dessert: it may sound unremarkable, but the chocolate cake with vanilla custard is sublime.

LASAI

Playful farm-to-fork fine dining

Rua Conde de Irajá, 191 (near Rua Capistrano de Abreu)
+55 21 3449 1834 / lasai.com.br / Closed Sunday and Monday

At Lasai, classic meals are creatively reinvented and given a cheeky, light-hearted treatment. Opened in 2014 by Rio native Chef Rafa Costa e Silva, who spent years training at influential Spanish restaurant Mugaritz, the whimsical plates – featuring produce grown in Rafa's own garden – immediately made a splash in the city's gastronomic scene. In its first year, Lasai placed 16th on the list of Latin America's 50 Best Restaurants – no mean feat. The space is spectacularly designed, and has a staff of 17 that serve a capacity of 26 diners. Expect 15-course tasting menus, bespoke tipples, sensational vegetarian options (a rarity here) and a hefty-but-worth-it bill to finish.

OLHO DA RUA

A multipurpose cultural space perfect for rainy days

Rua Bambina, 6 (near Rua Marquês de Olinda) / +55 21 3178 6601
olhodarua.com.br / Closed Sunday and Monday

They don't tell you this in the brochures, but it actually rains quite a lot here. While many people complain that there's nothing to do in the city when it's raining, I like to see what's going on at Olho da Rua, another of Botafogo's growing number of mixed-use spaces. There's an art gallery, a bar serving up top-notch artisanal beers, an area for artistic workshops and a performance space. It's worth checking their event listings before you set off, but with such wide variety of activities and shows, including art exhibitions, happy hours and live music, there's a good chance they'll always have something you like.

RESTAURANTE ADRIANO

Lunch with locals

Rua Real Grandeza, 162 (near Rua Voluntários da Pátria)
+55 21 2538 0825 / facebook.com/Restaurante-Adriano
Closed Sunday

When I was still new to Rio, one of my frustrations was that when I asked Cariocas for dining recommendations, they would send me to places they thought a foreigner would like instead of telling me where they like to go. Time and again, I found myself in overpriced, mediocre Italian eateries. What I really wanted was a place like Restaurante Adriano – it's a traditional spot where the menu hasn't changed much since opening in 1954. They serve up local eats like filé à Osvaldo Aranha, a juicy steak topped with crispy slivers of garlic that's named after a Brazilian politician and diplomat. This is a place to get under the skin of Rio, to rub shoulders with the locals.

WINEHOUSE

Informal bar do vinhos

Rua Paulo Barreto, 25 (near Rua Voluntários da Pátria)
+55 21 3264 4101 / winehouserio.com.br / Closed Sunday

Despite Brazil's proximity to Argentina and Chile, wine here has normally been a luxury reserved for the elite. This is reflected in wince-inducing prices and the dearth of anything decent sold by the glass. Step forward Dom and Selene – a wine-obsessed British-Brazilian couple who met during Carnival and eventually opened WineHouse, an oenophile's paradise without a trace of snobbery. In addition to an extensive catalog of bottles, there's also a blackboard listing around 10 wines sold by the glass, which changes regularly and always includes some Brazilian options. The comfortable interior and menu of delicious nibbles add to the relaxed atmosphere.

copacabana

Copacabana's star has faded since its 1930s heyday –
back then, the stunning crescent of golden sand was
a playground for the rich and famous. These days,
Copa's beach still draws large crowds on sunny
weekends, and also serves as the city's largest space
for al fresco events. The iconic wavy-patterned sidewalk
runs the length of the beach and is ideal for cyclists,
skaters and anyone who just enjoys walking and
people-watching. The blocks back from the beach may
look a little shabby in places, but push past the aging
tourist traps and you'll find hidden gems – bars and
family-run restaurants that pre-date the Second World
War. If you're looking for authentic, local experiences
with no frills, this is a rich hunting ground.

1   Adega Pérola
2   Boulangerie Guerin
3   Cervantes
4   Copacabana Palace Spa
5   Galeto Sat's
6   Gilson Martins
7   Pavão Azul

Cardeal Arcoverde

Praia de
Copacabana

ADEGA PÉROLA

Portuguese-style tapas

Rua Siqueira Campos, 138 (near Ladeira dos Tabajaras)
+55 21 2255 9425 / facebook.com/AdegaPerolaRiodeJaneiro
Closed Sunday

Though it doesn't look like much from the outside, this cozy bar gets so busy most nights of the week that the crowd often spills out onto the pavement. Step inside, and you'll see a long glass-sided counter running the length of the bar that houses a dazzling assortment of deli-style treats – marinated octopus, rollmops (pickled herring filets), olives, seafood escabeche; the list goes on and on. It may sound mad, but ignore the wines that line the walls, and opt for a draft beer or a caipirinha, as those are the drinks of choice here. During the dinner rush, expect to make some new friends as you'll most likely share your table with others.

BOULANGERIE GUERIN

Éclairs to clamor over

Avenida Nossa Senhora de Copacabana, 920 (near Rua Bolívar)
+55 21 2523 4140 / padariaguerin.com.br / Open daily

In early 2015, some shocking news spread through town, leading to cries of anguish: Boulangerie Guerin was closing. French pastry chef Dominique Guerin had opened his eponymous bakery three years earlier, and in that short time, it had won a legion of fans and multiple awards for its tasty bread, macarons and, perhaps most beloved of all, the divine éclairs. Thankfully, the despair of Rio's pastry lovers didn't last long. The same day that the distressing news was published in a local magazine, an investor swooped in to provide the funds needed to keep the business afloat. Guerin's éclairs live on, and they are a must, as is the luscious tartelette de framboesa, almond cake topped with fresh raspberries and a raspberry macaron lid.

CERVANTES

Epic late-night sandwiches

Avenida Prado Júnior, 335, Store B (at Rua Barata Riveiro)
+55 21 2275 6147 / restaurantecervantes.com.br / Open daily

This somewhat shabby bar opened in 1955, and judging by the interior, not much has changed since. Yet this is one of Copacabana's true jewels, full of history and tradition. A small bar leads on to a restaurant space crammed full of tables and chairs. Smart, experienced waiters in crisp white jackets move quickly between tables, expertly delivering foam-topped beers and fat sandwiches of juicy filet mignon and melting cheese, or roast pork with grilled pineapple. Since the '60s, this has been the venue of choice for late night drinkers, as it stays open until 4am during the week, and 6am on weekends.

COPACABANA PALACE SPA

A day of pampering in Rio's most storied hotel

Avenida Atlântica, 1702 (near Rua Rodolfo Dantas)
+55 21 2545 8787 / belmond.com/copacabana-palace-rio-de-janeiro
Open daily

The magnificent Art Deco façade of the Belmond Copacabana Palace is an impressive sight. Built in 1923, this grand hotel is steeped in infamy – Orson Welles notoriously trashed his room here, Errol Flynn supposedly danced naked down the hallways and Jayne Mansfield allegedly shocked the other guests by sunbathing topless by the pool. Today, the luxuries of this hotel are beyond most people's budgets, but if you'd like a taste, then try the day-use spa option available Monday through Thursday. Your day of being spoiled runs from 9am all the way until 8pm, and includes lunch at the relaxing Pérgula restaurant, access to the swimming pool and tennis courts, and a relaxing one-hour massage. Reservations must be made for this service, so if this sounds up your alley, be sure to book ahead.

GALETO SAT'S

Chefs' choice hangout for after-hours eating

Rua Barata Ribeiro, 7D (near Avenida Prado Júnior)
+55 21 2275 6197 / facebook.com/Galeto-Sats / Open daily

When Rio's hardworking chefs finish their long shifts, they make their way to Galeto Sat's, where the food is uncomplicated, satisfying and full of flavor, and the kitchen is open deep into the small hours of the night. The must-order here is galeto na brasa com farofa de ovo: chicken grilled over charcoal until crisp, served with a typical dish of egg and cassava flour. At 3am, Sérgio, the owner, clears the marble-topped bar of drinks and elbows, puts down a layer of flour and then lays out slices of complimentary pizza, which he bakes over a large charcoal grill. In addition to all that, Galeto Sat's also has a huge stock of cachaças and doesn't close until 5am, making this a fine spot for a saideira (nightcap) or to keep the party going.

GILSON MARTINS

Bold bags and wallets

Rua Figueiredo de Magalhães, 304 (near Rua Barata Ribeiro)
+55 21 3816 0552 / gilsonmartins.com.br / Closed Sunday

Most of the souvenirs peddled around town score low on both quality
and creativity. Who really needs another badly carved Christ the Redeemer
figure or cheap plastic keyring? If you want something eye-catching and
useful as a reminder of your time in Rio, then take a look at Gilson Martins'
iconic designs. The store stocks quality bags, purses, wallets, card holders,
luggage tags and laptop cases made of long-lasting materials like leather,
vinyl and canvas, and featuring clean, colorful designs. For a tasteful
memento, or a fashionably practical gift for friends, I recommend the line
of goods inspired by Brazil, from the country's flag to iconic landmarks, and
every Brazilian's obsession: soccer.

PAVÃO AZUL

Eat and drink with the locals

Rua Hilário de Gouvêia, 71 (at Rua Barta Ribeiro) / +55 21 2236 2381
facebook.com/pavaoazul / Open daily

If the thought of bars and restaurants designed to attract tourists
makes you shudder, then Pavão Azul is the place to go. This is the kind
of low-key bar that Cariocas love: a handful of simple tables and chairs
inside, a few more outside and five or six servers ferrying huge bottles
of beer – served up estupidamente gelada (stupidly cold), of course –
to customers. The menu is full of Brazilian comfort food – the divine
pataniscas de bacalhau (salted cod fritters) should not be missed.
On weekends, it gets busy and you may have to wait up to 30 minutes
for a table. Give the waiter your name, relax at one of the bar stools on
the sidewalk and he'll tell you when there's a seat free.

remote beaches

Where to go for a (nearly) private praia

PRAIA DE GRUMARI

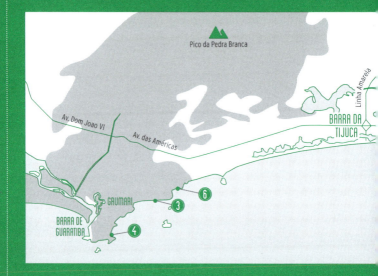

When it comes to praias (beaches), most people make a beeline for one of the big two: Ipanema and Copacabana. When they get there, however, they often find things are seriously overcrowded. Luckily, Rio has more than 40 other beaches to choose from, many of which will be far quieter. Note that the distant spots are best reached by car – hired cars are cheap, but you can also strike a deal with a local tour guide to take care of the transportation. Also, keep aware of your surroundings – I recommend traveling in a group and not lingering too long after sunset.

If you're looking to surf, you'll want to find your way to **Prainha** – you can either hail a cab or catch the Surfbus (surfbus.com.br), which runs daily from 7am to 7pm between Catete's Largo do Machado and Prainha. Prainha is particularly good for surfing due to its narrow stretch of sand bordered on both sides by large rocky outcrops that produce killer waves.

Map legend:

1 Ilha de Paquetá
2 Praia da Joatinga
3 Praia de Grumari
4 Praia do Perigoso
5 Praia Vermelha
6 Prainha

Only a few hundred meters past Prainha is **Praia de Grumari**. This 2.5 km (1.5 mile) stretch of pristine sand and crystal-clear water is located in a nature reserve, and is just the ticket if you like to have the beach all to yourself.

Another quiet option is Urca's **Praia Vermelha**, which is a 10-minute taxi ride from the hopping Copacabana beach. The small area doesn't get as packed as other central beaches and has extra options, such as sea kayaking or a tranquil walk around the base of nearby Sugarloaf Mountain.

Praia de Joatinga is a gorgeous beach, tucked away in the neighborhood of Joá. Be sure to check the tides before you go, though, as the shore disappears completely at high tide.

Praia do Perigoso is for the truly intrepid. In fact, it'd behoove you to consider hiring a guide, as this faraway area is reached after a one-hour coastal trek from Barra de Guaratiba on the far western outskirts of the city. Though it's not the easiest to get to, the picturesque white sands and turquoise water are quite the payoff.

Located in the middle of Guanabara Bay, sleepy little **Ilha de Paquetá** is barely over 2 km (around 1 mile) long, and reached via a scenic one-hour ferry ride from Praça XV de Novembro in Centro. The island has several beaches as well as a ban on all motor vehicles, so your transport options there are to walk, rent a bicycle, hire a bike taxi or, charmingly, a horse-drawn carriage, all of which can be arranged once you're on the island.

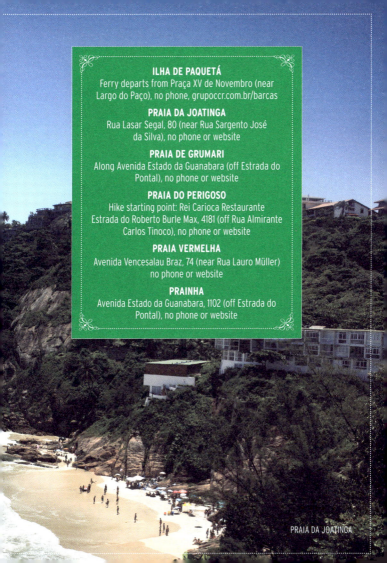

ILHA DE PAQUETÁ
Ferry departs from Praça XV de Novembro (near Largo do Paço), no phone, grupoccr.com.br/barcas

PRAIA DA JOATINGA
Rua Lasar Segal, 80 (near Rua Sargento José da Silva), no phone or website

PRAIA DE GRUMARI
Along Avenida Estado da Guanabara (off Estrada do Pontal), no phone or website

PRAIA DO PERIGOSO
Hike starting point: Rei Carioca Restaurante Estrada do Roberto Burle Max, 4181 (off Rua Almirante Carlos Tinoco), no phone or website

PRAIA VERMELHA
Avenida Vencesalau Braz, 74 (near Rua Lauro Müller) no phone or website

PRAINHA
Avenida Estado da Guanabara, 1102 (off Estrada do Pontal), no phone or website

PRAIA DA JOATINGA

ipanema
and leblon

For many visitors, simply the word "Ipanema" is enough to conjure up images of tall, tan beach beauties sashaying elegantly to a bossa nova soundtrack. While Ipanema and close neighbor Leblon certainly have their fair share of lithe bodies, what really sets this area apart is the money. This is where actors, politicians and athletes flock to enjoy the swankiest of everything that Rio has to offer: hotels, boutiques and restaurants – especially along Rua Dias Ferreira in Leblon. Along their shared southern edge, the two neighborhoods form one continuous stretch of sand, marked at one end by the twin mountains of Dois Irmãos and at the other by the rocks of Arpoador – a choice location for romantics who wait to applaud as the sun sinks below the horizon.

Ipanema/
General Osório

ILHA DOS
CAIÇARAS

ACADEMIA DA CACHAÇA

Quality feijoada and cachaça

Rua Conde de Bernadotte, 26 (near Rua Adalberto Ferreira)
+55 21 2239 1542 / academiadacachaca.com.br / Open daily

Feijoada, a hearty stew of meat and beans, is a Brazilian staple.
However, you should choose your restaurant wisely because after
you've plowed your way through this substantial meal, you won't want
to eat (or even move!) for a good, long time. So here's my recommendation:
get situated at Academia da Cachaça, which, in addition to a tremendous
feijoada, also has over 100 different brands of its eponymous spirit, and a
tasting menu of three different varieties, served neat, for the uninitiated.
Their Caipira Académica – a version of the famous cachaça-based
caipirinha – is not to be missed. All this comes in a refreshingly informal
atmosphere for upmarket Leblon.

CARAVANA HOLIDAY

Beach-chic women's fashion

Rua Aristídes Espínola, 121 (near Rua Dias Ferreira)
+55 21 2294 3998 / caravanaholiday.com / Closed Sunday

Many women visiting Rio find that, compared to the locals, their wardrobes are a little (how can I put this nicely?) muted. Though the fashion here is elegant, it's never demure – whether you're at the beach or out in the evening, you'll be surrounded by bright colors and loud patterns. Caravana Holiday carries a variety of brands inspired by the upscale Búzios beach resort, a popular vacation destination located on a peninsula east of Rio. With lightweight dresses, attractive hats, silk shirts, shoes and other accessories, this store is your shortcut to dressing – and perhaps feeling – like a Carioca.

CARE BODY & SOUL

Luxury spa and high-end hairdressing

Rua Barão de Jaguaripe, 289 (near Rua Garcia d'Avila) / **+55 21 3813 0560**
salaocare.com.br / **Closed Sunday**

The pure white, minimalist exterior of Care Body & Soul gives you an idea of what to expect inside – a grand and tranquil haven, away from the stress of the raucous city. The impressive choice of treatments available includes massages, manicures and pedicures, facials and makeup services, eyebrow shaping, and, of course, waxing. This is Brazil after all! Above all, though, this day spa is known for its hair salon, providing glorious cuts, coloring and all sorts of treatments, ranging from smoothing to relaxing to conditioning. If you're fair complected, consider their lauded spray-tan treatment – it takes 60 seconds and lasts 10 days.

CONFEITARIA KURT

Rio's oldest bakery

Rua General Urquiza, 117, Store B (near Rua Professor Artur Ramos)
+55 21 2294 0599 / confeitariakurt.com.br / Closed Sunday

In 1939, Kurt Deichmann escaped Nazi Germany and made his way to Rio.
Three years later, he opened this now-famous cake shop. Today, his niece,
Evelyn, runs the show and ensures that the practices her uncle insisted
upon — fresh ingredients and great customer service — are retained.
The two essential cakes to try have been on the menu from the very
beginning: picada de abelha (also called the bienenstich, or "bee sting
cake") has layers of sponge and vanilla cream topped with crunchy
honeycomb, and torta de damasco, an apricot and whipped cream cake.
On weekends, you may see Evelyn carrying on another of her uncle's
traditions: handing out cookies to kids passing by the bakery.

CT BOUCHERIE

Elevated experience for carnivores

Rua Dias Ferreira, 636 (near Rua General Urquiza)
+55 21 2529 2329 / **ctboucherie.com.br** / **Open daily**

If you're a serious meat lover, CT Boucherie needs to be at the top of your where-to-eat list when you're in town. Actually, even if you're a vegetarian, you might want to check it out. The restaurant flips the all-you-can-eat, quantity-over-quality, Brazilian churrascaria format on its head: first, select a single piece of meat from the mouth-watering selection — I can tell you from experience that the bone-in prime rib is outstanding. As you enjoy your meaty centerpiece, you will be continually presented with items from a dazzling variety of never-ending meat-free sides — ratatouille, cauliflower cheese and divine potatoes dauphinoise were highlights of my most recent visit. Additionally, a wide array of vegetarian appetizers, salads and fish options are available, and there's a solid wine list — friendly to every diet I'm aware of — which is dominated by French and Argentinian reds.

MARIA OITICICA BIOJÓIAS

Amazonian bio-jewelry

**Avenida Afrânio de Melo Franco, 290, Store 112B (near Rua Professor
Antônio Maria Teixeira) / +55 21 3875 8025 / oja.mariaoiticica.com.br
Open daily**

I'm not a fan of malls, but, in Rio, sometimes the stores housed inside them
go far beyond the typical chains. While most of us think of the Amazon
rainforest as a haven of wildlife, Maria Oiticica sees something else – raw
materials for biojóias, or bio-jewelry, pieces made from natural materials.
Having grown up in the heart of the Amazon, Maria knows firsthand what to
source: seeds, pods, bark, leaves and straw, among others. She works directly
with indigenous cooperatives to purchase her materials, and puts a strong
emphasis on sustainability and social responsibility. Her creations – jewelry
and other accessories, such as handbags and keychains – are often bold and
always unconventional.

MIL FRUTAS CAFÉ

Gourmet ice cream

Rua Garcia d'Avila, 134, Store A (near Rua Barão da Torre)
+55 21 2521 1384 / milfrutas.com.br / Open daily

Mil Frutas translates as "one thousand fruits", but I'm sure you'll forgive the exaggeration once you see the incredible variety of ice cream and sorbet flavors here, which actually comes to just over 200, all made with natural ingredients. On the more obscure side are Amazonian fruits such as cupuaçu, a fruit that tastes of melon, pineapple and vodka, and the sweet-and-sour bacuri; herbal aromatics like chamomile and jasmine; and alcoholic options such as absinthe, Champagne and saké. Unless you're absolutely certain you know what you want, take your time to browse the options – you're allowed three provas (tastes) before you commit to an order. Use them wisely!

POLIS SUCOS

Rio's original juice bar

Rua Maria Quitéria, 70 (near Rua Visconde de Pirajá)
+55 21 2247 2518 / polissucos.com.br / Open daily

Juice bars are not solely for my-body-is-a-temple health-obsessives here – they are a part of everyday life for everyone from construction workers to executives. Today, you'll find juiceries scattered all over the city, but Polis Sucos lays claim to being the first. The corner store opened in 1958 and is easily recognizable with its iconic red sign in the heart of Ipanema, which is the perfect place to lure in beachgoers after an arduous day of tanning and volleyball. Unlike most juice bars, Polis doesn't use frozen pulp – only fresh fruit, which you can see lined up at the counter. Try the zingy fruta do conde (custard apple) or my wife's pick, mamão com laranja (papaya with orange).

Q CHOCOLATE

Confections for grown-ups

Rua Garcia D'Ávila, 149, Store B (near Rua Redentor)
+55 21 2523 5009 / chocolateq.com / Closed Sunday

Despite being one of the world's largest producers of cocoa, most of Brazil's everyday chocolate is unlikely to impress a true connoisseur. Thankfully, chocoholics do have one serious option here: Q Chocolate. The store's flagship location is fitting for such a posh brand – right in the very middle of Ipanema. Inside, the grandeur continues – dark wood paneling and attractive packaging featuring Audubon-style illustrations of local wildlife. The Aquim family works to highlight the cocoa bean in every piece sold by using only three ingredients: cocoa liquor, cocoa butter and sugar. The chocolate itself comes from a single farm in the Brazilian Atlantic rainforest, and is made without any artificial additives. If, like me, you're a dark chocolate fan, don't miss the bars ranging from 55% to 85% cocoa.

TOCA DO VINICIUS

Bastion of bossa nova

Rua Vinícius de Moraes, 129 (near Rua Barão da Torre)
+55 21 2522 4993 / facebook.com/tocadovinicius / Open daily

The rise of bossa nova in the 1950s helped create the idea of Rio as a city simultaneously sophisticated and laid-back; exotic and effortlessly cool. Sadly, enthusiasm for the genre has faded, and there are now just a handful of devotees, such as Toca do Vinicius storeowner Carlos Alberto Afonso, who we can thank for keeping Rio's bossa nova scene alive. Carlos opened the shop in 1993, and his love and devotion to bossa nova is plain to see. The thing he created has become many things: dusty old record store, museum and library. On Sundays, the store occasionally hosts spellbinding live performances with audiences spilling out the doors.

ZAZÁ BISTRÔ TROPICAL

Delicious fusion

Rua Joana Angélica, 40 (at Rua Prudente de Morais)
+55 21 2247 9101 / zazabistro.com.br / Open daily

Situated a mere block from the beach, the draw of this much-loved
Ipanema restaurant starts with the inventive cocktails. The menu, like
the décor, is an exquisite and eclectic mix of Brazilian, North African and
Southeast Asian influences, with an emphasis on fruit and seafood.
If you want a place on Zazá's coveted veranda, most evenings you'll need
to book ahead or expect a long wait, though during the hotter months,
many opt for the air-conditioned comfort of the interior spaces, which
include a Middle Eastern-inspired room on the second floor, strewn with
lavish cushions and thick rugs.

RIO BY BIKE

adventure time

Trek, skate, bike, climb and glide

CACHOEIRA DOS PRIMATAS
Trail begins: Rua Sara Viléla, 500 (near Rua Visconde de Itaúna), etrilhas.com.br, open daily

COMPANHIA DA ESCALADA
Address varies by course, +55 21 2567 7105
companhiadaescalada.com.br, open daily

ESTILO VOO LIVRE
Estrada das Canoas, 722 (near Caminho da Canoa)
+55 21 99862 7104, estilovoolivre.com, open daily

GUANABARA LONGBOARD ESCOLA
Avenida Infante Dom Henrique (near Marina da Gloría), +55 21 99833 7421, guanabaraboards.com
open daily

RIO BY BIKE
Meeting point varies by tour, +55 21 96871 8933
riobybike.com, open daily

SURF'SUP
Meeting point varies by lesson, +55 21 99214 0797
surfsuprio.com, open daily

Rio's dramatic combination of mountains, forests and coastlines pretty much demands that you get out there and enjoy it. Whether you like your activities with plenty of adrenaline or prefer something more laid-back, there are lots of options here.

Run by Dutch journalists Philip and Jan, the outstanding **Rio By Bike** offers daily bike tours (yes, the bikes are provided) conducted in English, Portuguese or Dutch. The tour covers routes through the beach neighborhoods as well as the historic city center, and is a great way for visitors to get a feel for the town.

Rio's parks, boardwalks, gentle slopes and growing network of cycling paths have fueled a huge growth in the longboarding scene recently. **Guanabara Longboard Escola** in Gloría teaches lessons for all ages and levels of experience, and has boards for rent.

From lagoons and protected bays to beaches with world-class surfing, Rio is blessed with a long and varied coastline. Stand-up paddling (SUP) is a great (and far less strenuous!) alternative, if you're not one for surfing. **Surf'Sup** has all the equipment and expertise to get you started — simply let them know which beach you prefer and they'll bring everything to you.

Given that the Tijuca Forest covers a huge area of the city, hiking opportunities abound. While serious hikes are best undertaken with an experienced guide, if you want an easy, scenic route that doesn't require assistance to navigate, the 30-minute forest trail to the **Cachoeira dos Primatas** waterfall can be followed independently, and makes a refreshing change from a day at the beach.

If you're here to do some proper mountain climbing, try scaling Pão de Açúcar (Sugarloaf Mountain). The only way to reach the top is by climbing, though there is a cable car if you're feeling lazy. Rock climbing school **Companhia da Escalada** hosts classes for beginners and experts on Sugarloaf's established routes, and has equipment and guides if you want to take on any of the city's other peaks.

Perhaps the ultimate way to appreciate the beauty of Rio is to look down on it from above. **Estilo Voo Livre** takes guests on tandem hang-gliding and paragliding flights from Pedra Bonita, a flight-path that affords breathtaking views of forests, favelas, mountains and beaches.

ESTILO VOO LIVRE

jardim botânico

gávea, lagoa

The posh neighborhoods of Lagoa, Jardim Botânico and Gávea, located between the beach neighborhoods of Leblon and Ipanema and up to the base of the dramatic Corcovado Mountain, are home to some of the city's most exclusive shops and fine dining restaurants. However, visitors pinching their pennies still have plenty of reasons to visit as many of the biggest attractions are free. Lagoa's titular Lagoa Rodrigo de Freitas, a large saltwater lagoon, is ringed by 7.5 km (4.5 miles) of cycling lanes, and the waterside views of Christ the Redeemer and the mountains always make this a busy spot at sunset. Jardim Botânico, located directly north of the eponymous gardens, is a great place to de-stress while strolling down avenues populated with monkeys and tropical birds. To the west, Gávea is mostly residential, but provides lively and affordable nightlife options thanks to the students from the nearby university.

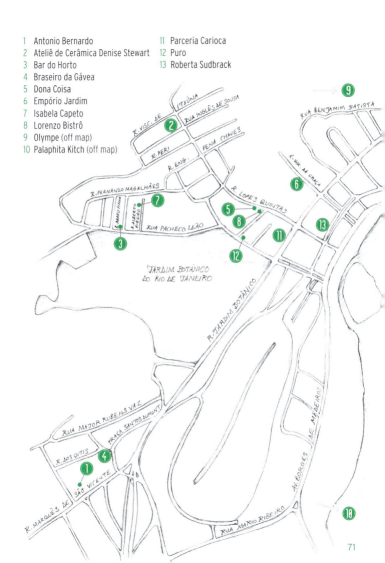

1 Antonio Bernardo
2 Ateliê de Cerâmica Denise Stewart
3 Bar do Horto
4 Braseiro da Gávea
5 Dona Coisa
6 Empório Jardim
7 Isabela Capeto
8 Lorenzo Bistrô
9 Olympe (off map)
10 Palaphita Kitch (off map)
11 Parceria Carioca
12 Puro
13 Roberta Sudbrack

ANTONIO BERNARDO

Whimsical jewelry and accessories

Rua Marquês de São Vicente, 52, Store 330 (near Rua das Acácias)
+55 21 2274 7796 / **antoniobernardo.com.br** / **Open daily**

A native of Rio, Antonio Bernardo traveled to Switzerland when he was 21 to learn the craft of watchmaking. Some years later, he returned home and studied to be a goldsmith before opening his eponymous shop in Gávea. Antonio now works primarily with gold and silver, creating rings, necklaces, earrings and cufflinks. His main inspiration is to give his pieces a sense of movement, and this is reflected in his novel use of threads, plates, color and jewels. Some of his most notable pieces also show a playful quality, as evidenced by his eight-part puzzle rings, which must be assembled afresh each time they are worn.

ATELIÊ DE CERÂMICA
DENISE STEWART

Snazzy pottery

Rua Inglês de Souza, 274 (near Rua Lopes Quintas)
+55 21 2294 4698 / denisestewart.com.br / By appointment

Denise Stewart started working with ceramics in 1997 and only two years later, opened her studio and store in Horto (the higher, more exclusive part of Jardim Botânico). Stewart creates plates, water jugs, serving bowls, vases, tea sets and some purely artistic objects. Over the years, she has developed a wide range of styles – I gravitate toward the dinnerware made in muted browns, blues and grays. However, not everything is understated: Denise also uses patterns of repeated horizontal stripes in primary colors as well as black-and-white polka dots and checkerboard patterns. Considering that this is the artist's studio, as well as a store, be sure to call ahead to arrange a visit in advance.

BAR DO HORTO

Quirky bar serving local fare

Rua Pacheco Leão, 780 (near Rua Abreu Fialho) / **+55 21 3114 8439**
facebook.com/Bar-Do-Horto / **Closed Monday**

Located just across the road from the Botanical Gardens, Bar do Horto is housed in a lovely green mansion with arched windows. Inside, there's a kaleidoscopic riot of color – the wall behind the bar is a melange of floral patterns, and a multitude of vibrant-hued lamps hang from the ceiling. The drinks tend to be fun and fruity, and all the old favorites can be found on the drink list alongside cheeky house concoctions like the refreshing caipilé, made with vodka and a whole fruit popsicle dunked in the glass. As for food, it's classic Brazilian grub here, so get your fill of feijão amigo (black bean soup), sardinha crocante (crispy fried sardines) and the impressive camarão cremoso (a creamy shrimp stew served in a hollowed out pumpkin) while listening to live acoustic tunes.

BRASEIRO DA GÁVEA

Post-soccer steaks and beers

Praça Santos Dumont, 116 (near Rua dos Oitis) / **+55 21 2239 7494**
braseirodagavea.com.br / **Open daily**

This much-loved, unassuming steakhouse is the centerpiece of Baixo
Gávea, a small group of bars and restaurants housed along Praça Santos
Dumont that is popular with residents of the neighborhood. Things tend
to get very rowdy here after soccer matches so you may have to wait for a
table, but once seated, you have some essential orders: start with chope
(the word for a draft beer in Brazil) and linguiça (a sausage served straight
from the huge charcoal grill); for the main event, the compulsory order is
picanha ao braseiro, a massive, juicy steak that will easily feed two, served
with broccoli rice and toothsome farofa de ovo (eggs scrambled with
cassava flour).

DONA COISA

Fashion boutique and household decorations

Rua Lopes Quintas, 153 (near Rua Visconde de Carandaí)
+55 21 2249 2336 / donacoisa.com.br / Closed Sunday

Dona Coisa is my port of call when I'm shopping for the women in my life. The pure white interior of this two-story house is split into several different areas, each a rich hunting ground for the desirable and gift worthy. Owner Roberta Damasceno and her team have carefully selected the items, as evidenced by the sheer quality and variety of goods. The ground floor features racks and shelves displaying dresses, shoes and accessories, mostly from local designers like Gloria Coelho and Adriana Degreas, as well as décor such as vases, photo frames and scrapbooks. Up on the second floor, you'll find books, fresh flowers, and a café and bar (try the gourmet brownies) if all that shopping works up an appetite.

EMPÓRIO JARDIM

The ultimate in breakfast and brunch

Rua Visconde da Graça, 51 (near Rua Jardim Botânico)
+55 21 2535 9862 / emporiojardimrio.com.br / **Open daily**

Empório Jardim has been lauded as the best place for breakfast in Rio, and deservedly so. The interior is funky – eye-catching cushions are scattered around banquettes, providing a nice contrast with the whitewashed wood chairs and polished concrete flooring. If you fancy something healthy, you have plenty of options – housemade yogurt with granola and seasonal fruits sourced from local markets, various salads and freshly squeezed juices (I love the pineapple juice served with fresh mint). If you prefer the more indulgent route then there are dozens of rich, delectable options, like buttery croissants filled with slabs of melting brie, croque madame and the unmissable gougères, melt-in-your-mouth, bite-sized breads made with gruyère. If you want to turn it into a boozy brunch, then try the refreshing bellinis or the Jardim do Rei, a mojito made with coconut water.

ISABELA CAPETO

Ritzy handmade women's fashion

Rua Alberto Ribeiro, 17 (near Rua Pacheco Leão) / **+55 21 2537 3331**
isabelacapeto.com.br / **Closed Saturday and Sunday**

Isabela Capeto is undoubtedly one of Brazil's most exclusive designers. After graduating from Accademia Italiana in Florence, Isabela returned home to Rio and opened her atelier in 2002. Located on a calm residential street in Horto, the studio is spacious and homey, with hardwood floors, worn leather sofas and a kitchen off to one side (which Isabela has been known to use for baking cakes to serve guests). The care and attention that go into her creations are evident – dresses, jackets and accessories are often embellished with hand-stitched appliqués. The impressive designs and high-quality craftsmanship are reflected in the prices, but an Isabela Capeto piece is something that will last, and be treasured, for years.

LORENZO BISTRÔ

French-Italian comfort food

Rua Visconde de Carandaí, 2 (at Rua Lopes Quintas)
+55 21 2294 7830 / lorenzobistro.com.br / Open daily

Lorenzo Bistrô is a good idea any time of day. The menu combines
French staples like salade Niçoise and cassoulet with Italian-inspired
risottos and pastas, and the tiled floors, solid wooden furniture and
sumptuously thick white tablecloths give Lorenzo the air of a Parisian
café. I've yet to visit without ordering the divine polenta do Lulu,
a combination of creamy polenta, truffled mushrooms and a soft egg
yolk. The whole roast chicken with porcini mushrooms and caramelized
onions is also blissful. The adjoining Casa Carandaí delicatessen, operated
by the same team, has terrific lunch options, many of which come in at
under R$40 (around US$10).

OLYMPE

French-Brazilian haute cuisine

Rua Custódio Serrão, 62 (near Rua Frei Leandro) / +55 21 2537 8582
olympe.com.br / Closed Sunday

French chef Claude Troisgros and his son Thomas come from an illustrious culinary family – Claude's father and uncle, among others, are credited with inventing nouvelle cuisine back in the '60s. Today, chefs Claude and Thomas work at Olympe, the benchmark against which the city's posh restaurants are measured. The concept is to apply French cooking techniques to Brazilian ingredients, and the results are spectacular: I fell in love with the giant ravioli stuffed with batata baroa mousse, and the foie gras and heart of palm terrine served with rapadura shavings was unforgettable. In addition to the à la carte menu, there are two tasting menu options – the five-course client's choice menu and a seven-course chef's menu, as well as an option for vegetarians. Toward the end of evening service, both chefs often make their rounds to greet guests.

PALAPHITA KITCH

Romantic setting for a sundowner

Avenida Epitácio Pessoa s/n (near Avenida Henrique Dodsworth)
+55 21 2227 0837 / palaphitakitch.com.br / Open daily

With its grass huts and chunky wooden furniture, Palaphita Kitch conjures up images of tropical safaris and jungle lodges. Located on the beachy southeast bank of Rodrigo de Freitas Lagoa, the view takes in the dramatic mountains, and the reflections on the water at sunset make for a truly magical experience. Arrive early to snag an elevated bench table, which is reached by ladder, then pick your poison from the extensive drink list; many of them involve Amazonian fruits, like the capivara, made with cupuaçu. As the sun dips below the horizon, waiters light the bamboo torches dotted around the grounds, casting a flickering glow across the space. On a warm, clear evening, there is surely no more idyllic spot in the city.

PARCERIA CARIOCA

Funky clothes and fun accessories

Rua Jardim Botânico, 728, Store 108 (near Rua Lopes Quintas)
+55 21 2259 1437 / facebook.com/parceria.carioca / Closed Sunday

When Flavia Torres started teaching jewelry making and design to students in disadvantaged communities, she found that although her students graduated with valuable skills, they often couldn't find stockists for their products. She solved this problem by opening Parceria Carioca. Today, this neat little shop is packed with striking handmade items – T-shirts, jewelry, flip-flops, beach bags and toys and games for younger children. The focus on light-hearted, contemporary design makes this a choice place to shop with (or for) children and young adults. The fact that all products are designed and manufactured locally as part of a scheme that supports young artisans should be a very pleasing bonus.

PURO

Upscale fare with a distinctive taste of Brazil

Rua Visconde de Carandaí, 43 (near Rua Pacheco Leão)
+55 21 3284 5377 / purorestaurante.com.br / Open daily

Foodie hearts skipped a beat when Chef Pedro Siqueira – who worked in such highly acclaimed restaurants as Taillevent in Paris and DOM in São Paulo – opened Puro in March 2015. For all the expectations given Siqueira's pedigree, Puro doesn't disappoint. If the rave reviews don't convince you, consider this: even my mother was impressed! Set in a 20th-century mansion, Puro's design is eccentric – spools of multi-colored yarn adorn the white walls and the back-lit bar gives a hint of the magnificent creations. And the food? It's some of the most innovative I've tasted. Uniquely Brazilian ingredients are taken in unexpected and delicious directions such as pupunha (hearts of palm) fashioned into ravioli, or pão de queijo (Brazilian cheese bread) stuffed with succulent pulled pork and microherbs.

ROBERTA SUDBRACK

Plates from a star local chef

**Avenida Lineu de Paula Machado, 916
(near Rua Saturnino de Brito)
+55 21 3874 0139
robertasudbrack.com.br
Closed Sunday and Monday**

Roberta Sudbrack started out selling hot dogs on the streets of Brasília, and worked her way up to being personal chef for the President of Brazil from 1996–2003. Since then, she's been named the best female chef in the region by Latin America's 50 Best Restaurants, and her eponymous restaurant has been ranked higher than any other restaurant in Rio. What I find most exciting about her cooking is that she transforms everyday fruits and vegetables into something magical and unexpected. I was never a big fan of okra until I tried her smoked okra and shrimp topped with caviar-like okra seeds – it was a revelation. This experience doesn't come cheap, but if inventive fine dining is your thing, then this is a compulsory stop.

zona oeste

barra da tijuca, barra de guaratiba, joá, vargem grande, vidigal

Before the Olympics, Rio's vast Zona Oeste (West Zone) rarely made it onto most visitors' radar: it's a minimum 30-minute taxi ride from the city center and, until recently, had limited public transport options. With the 2016 Summer Olympic Village centered around Barra da Tijuca, the area has seen significant developments with the addition of event venues for the global games as well as leisure parks, arts spaces and neighborhood upgrades. So if you're willing to venture beyond tourist-friendly Zona Sul (South Zone), you'll find nature reserves and pristine beaches in neighborhoods Barra de Guaratiba and Grumari, and Floresta da Tijuca, one of the world's largest urban forests and a hiker's dream. Then there's Pedra Bonita, the preferred jump-off point for hang-gliders. But that's not all: there are also splendid restaurants and bars with glorious views, romantic getaways and niche shops. With a new metro line and dedicated high-speed bus lanes, going west is becoming much easier.

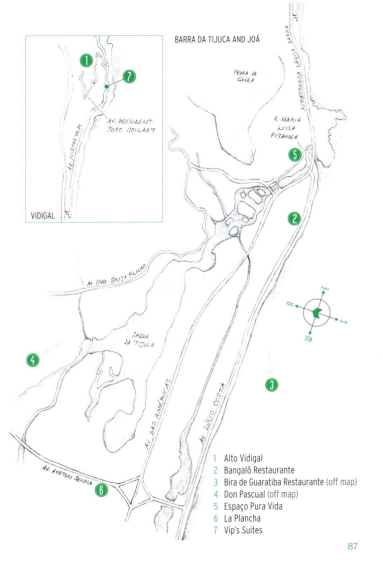

BARRA DA TIJUCA AND JOÁ

VIDIGAL

1 Alto Vidigal
2 Bangalô Restaurante
3 Bira de Guaratiba Restaurante (off map)
4 Don Pascual (off map)
5 Espaço Pura Vida
6 La Plancha
7 Vip's Suites

ALTO VIDIGAL

Favela bar with a stunning view

Rua Armando de Almeida Lima, 2 (near Rua 25 de Outubro)
+55 21 98741 3036 / facebook.com/altovidigal / Closed Monday

While many of Rio's favelas still have serious problems with crime and sanitation, several have become increasingly safe for visitors in recent years, as in the case of Vidigal, thanks to its relative proximity to Leblon (still, be mindful of your surroundings). Alto Vidigal is a basic bar attached to a hostel located right at the very top of the favela – the drinks and pub grub are certainly fine, but you really come here for the mind-blowing view. The fastest way to reach the bar is to take a cheap mini-van or motorcycle taxi (the latter is best for adrenaline junkies) from Avenida Niemeyer up through the steep, narrow streets. It's also a good place for a pit stop after the trek down from the nearby Dois Irmãos peak (see pg 126).

BANGALÔ RESTAURANTE

Beachfront seafood and music

Avenida Lucio Costa, 1976 (near Rua Professor Coutinho Fróis)
+55 21 2493 0313 / facebook.com/Bangalô-Restaurante / Open daily

Bangalô (that's "bungalow" in Portuguese) is a charming bar and restaurant facing the beach in Barra da Tijuca. The interior features light wood paneling and seagrass, which helps create a laid-back, informal atmosphere that matches the beachside location. The menu is dominated by excellent seafood, and the polvo assado (roasted octopus) is a must. The drinks menu includes beers and mainstay cocktails, but the highlight is the range of caipirinhas made with exotic fruits. The regular live music performances between 7–10pm are enjoyable, but tend to be quite loud, so avoid visiting during those hours if you want to have a conversation while you eat.

BIRA DE GUARATIBA RESTAURANTE

Upmarket food with a killer view

Estrada da Vendinha, 68, Store A (near Rua Cleber de Souza Siqueira)
**+55 21 2410 8304 / restaurantedobira.com.br / Open Thursday
through Sunday**

In 1991, local fisherman Bira decided to turn his house into a seafood
restaurant. The rustic space, dominated by huge wooden verandas, is only
open four days a week, and the remote neighborhood of Barra de Guaratiba
takes at least an hour by car to reach from central Rio. So why do people
bother? Bira de Guaratiba Restaurante is the definition of destination dining
– sitting high on a hill overlooking the pristine Restinga da Marambaia
reserve, the scenery is breathtaking, and when the huge clay pot of still-
bubbling moqueca (seafood stew) arrives at your table, you'll know the
trip was worth it.

DON PASCUAL

Picturesque forest hideaway

Estrada do Sacarrão, 867 (at Caminho do Sacarrão)
+55 21 2428 6237 / donpascual.com.br / Open daily

Don Pascual is a restaurant for hopeless romantics; for those who value magic and adventure over everyday convenience. The lengthy journey (30 minutes west from Barra da Tijuca) means you'll need to rent a car or hire a taxi, and takes you into Vargem Grande, a tranquil neighborhood in the depths of Tijuca Forest. The large wooden house is surrounded by gardens, which are lit up brilliantly at night. Sit out on the shaded decks in the garden or, on chillier winter evenings, snuggle up near the open fire inside. The menu includes handmade pizzas and some first-rate seafood options such as the savory spaghetti aos frutos do mar (seafood spaghetti) and polvo do Don (grilled octopus with asparagus). Book ahead, and allow yourself plenty of time to enjoy the enchanting atmosphere.

ESPAÇO PURA VIDA

Healthful activities and bites by the beach

Rua Maria Luísa Pitanga, 163 (near Estrada do Joá)
+55 21 99539 6117 / facebook.com/espacopuravidaa / Open daily

Most of Rio's oceanfront kiosks serve up cheap fried food and are plastered with gaudy adverts for beer and soda, but not every place is like that. After a serious car accident in 2011, Pedro Pires retired from modeling and decided to create a different kind of beach-side experience. He left behind the excesses of his party lifestyle and opened Espaço Pura Vida, which translates to "pure living space", in Joá. Here, you can practice yoga, attend a meditation session, join Pedro for a surf lesson or head out on a SUP (stand-up paddle) board. In addition to the mindfulness and water sports, this is also a restaurant with a menu of fresh juices and satisfying vegetarian meals.

LA PLANCHA

Seafood extravaganza in the fish market

Avenida Ayrton Senna, 5500 (near Avenida Tenente Coronel Muniz de Aragão) / +55 21 3325 3383 / laplancha.com.br / Open daily

Seafood restaurants located in (or even close to) fish markets always give me a bit of a thrill. One thing you can almost always guarantee is that the ingredients are fresh, and with seafood, that's half the battle won. La Plancha opened in the main fish market in Barra da Tijuca in 1994, and quickly impressed the locals with a menu of daily catches stuffed full of Spanish and Brazilian flavors. Though a recent refurbishment has reduced the number of seats in the restaurant, it's still worth waiting in line for their crowd-pleasing parrillada de frutos do mar, a massive array of grilled seafood including lobster and monstrous shrimps.

VIP'S SUITES

Rooms designed for romance

Avenida Niemeyer, 418 (near Estrada da Gávea) / **+55 21 3322 1662**
vipsmotel.com.br / **Open daily**

Because most Brazilians don't move out of their parents' home until well past university age, there is a thriving market for amorous getaways for affluent 20- and 30-something couples. But if the phrase "love hotel" conjures up seedy images of shabby motel rooms, then Vip's (pronounced phonetically rather than according to acronym) will make you think again. Their suites, hired in eight-hour blocks, are immaculately fitted with huge beds (naturally), private saunas, hot tubs and massive private terraces with swimming pools and marvelous sea views. This can be a fun and very Brazilian way to spice up a holiday, but all those fancy amenities mean that the suites are often sought after as risqué party venues, too.

RIO AFTER DARK:
watering holes

Botecos, botequins and bares

BAR DOS DESCASADOS

ALFA BAR
Rua Mena Barreto, 94 (near Rua Sorocaba)
+55 21 2266 2510, wikirio.com.br/Alfa_Bar, open daily

BAR D'HÔTEL
Avenida Delfim Moreira, 696 (near Avenida
Bartolomeu Mitre), +55 21 2172 1112
hoteismarina.com.br, open daily

BAR DO MINEIRO
Rua Paschoal Carlos Magno, 99 (near Rua Fonseca
Guimarães), +55 21 2221 9227, bardomineiro.net
open daily

BAR DOS DESCASADOS
R. Alm. Alexandrino, 660 (near Rua Aprazível)
+55 21 2222 2755, santa-teresa-hotel.com
open daily

CANASTRA BAR
Rua Jangadeiros, 42 (near Rua Visconde de Pirajá)
+55 21 99656 1960, facebook.com/Canastra-Bar
closed Sunday and Monday

It might be the beaches, mountains and Carnival that make the brochures, but Rio's bars deserve more than your passing attention. Cariocas refer affectionately to several different grades of bar, from pé sujos (slang for a dive bar that means "dirty foot"), to botecos, botequins and bares. The difference between the latter three is nuanced, but if you're truly curious and have 20 minutes to spare, ask a friendly local to explain.

Bar do Mineiro ("Mineiro" for short) is one of Santa Teresa's two most known and loved old bars (the other being Armazém São Thiago, see pg 13), and is a great place to sample one of Rio's tastiest feijoadas. On weekends, this becomes a hive of social activity, with a young, bohemian crowd that fills the pavement and spills out onto the road outside the packed interior. Fun fact: there are no restrictions about drinking on the street here.

BAR DO MINEIRO

Bar dos Descasados is just a short walk from Mineiro, but at the other end of the scale in terms of luxury. Attached to the five-star Hotel Santa Teresa, this elegant space has original exposed brick arches, four-poster sofa loungers and fabulous views across the treetops. Stop in for a few posh cocktails – my recommendation is the watermelon and lemongrass caipirinha.

Ipanema has its share of overpriced tourist traps, but **Canastra Bar**, opened in 2015 by a trio of French friends, has quickly gained fans. This unpretentious wine bar with sidewalk seating offers a handful of affordable Brazilian wines by the glass, and delicious platters of cheese and ham.

Only a few steps from Leblon beach, **Bar d'Hôtel** is where to go for swanky, creative tipples. Chief barman, Tai Barbin, serves up exquisite creations such as the Alem das Nuvens ("Beyond the Clouds"), a blend of aged rum, red berries and Grand Marnier, topped with a dreamy maple syrup foam.

If you're more interested in socializing than fancy drinks, head to Botafogo's **Alfa Bar.** This casual boteco attracts droves of young revelers who pack the walkway as they down ice-cold beers and fill the air with lively chit-chat. It's the perfect place to start the night before heading across the road to Comuna (see pg 30) for boozy drinks and award-winning burgers.

RIO AFTER DARK:
samba spots

Dance to the beat

BAR BIP BIP
Rua Almirante Gonçalves, 50 (near Rua Aires de
Saldanha), +55 21 2267 9656
facebook.com/barbipbip, open daily

BAR SEMENTE
Rua Evaristo da Veiga, 149 (near Rua Joaquim Silva)
no phone, facebook.com/barsemente, open daily

PEDRA DO SAL
Rua Argemiro Bulcão, 1 (near Rua São Francisco
da Prainha), +55 21 99659 2211
facebook.com/rodadesambapedradosal
open Monday

SAMBA DO OUVIDOR
Rua do Ouvidor, 1 (near Rua do Mercado), no phone
sambadaouvidor.blogspot.com.br, open Saturday

TRAPICHE GAMBOA
Rua Sacadura Cabral, 155 (near Rua Camerino)
+55 21 2516 0868, trapichegamboa.com
closed Sunday and Monday

In today's world of fast-moving trends, it's impressive to see how popular samba is with young and old alike. This music and dance, though rooted in Africa, emerged in Rio at the beginning of the 20th century and is still very much alive. Visiting here without at least listening to some samba would be to miss out on an important (and fun!) part of the city's culture.

The quilombo (African settlement) of Saúde, just north of Centro, is nicknamed "the cradle of samba". Though the somewhat run-down neighborhood isn't where you'd normally want to be after dark, the town square comes alive every Monday evening for the outdoor **Pedra do Sal** event from 7pm until midnight. It's typically a relaxed, informal affair with street vendors selling beer and snacks, and musicians playing as they sit around a few tables. Revelers dance in the square or sit on the large rock that overlooks the scene. Be sure to check the forecast though, as it's canceled in the event of heavy rain.

On Friday and Saturday nights, **Trapiche Gamboa** – also in Saúde – is hands down my favorite samba club in Rio. This lovingly restored building comprises a large dance floor and bar, overlooked by two mezzanine levels, ideal for surveying the scene if dancing isn't your thing. Amazing samba bands quickly have the space packed with talented dancers doing astounding things with their feet.

Another samba street party is **Samba do Ouvidor**, which runs from 5pm every Saturday on Centro's Rua do Ouvidor, one of the oldest roads in the city. This part of the street is pedestrianized and home to several pleasing bars, giving you the option to take a break and grab a bite when fatigue sets in.

While most samba venues center on dancing, **Bar Semente** is an intimate Lapa venue where guests book tables and watch musical performances up close from the comfort of their chairs. This being Brazil, some people can't help themselves and will get up and have a little shimmy, but this is a significantly more laid-back experience.

Similarly, music is the main event at Copacabana's **Bar Bip Bip**, which hosts regular samba and chorinho (a gentler variation of samba) nights. Cariocas are passionate about samba, and beloved owner Alfredo is perhaps even more so, as his love for the music means the musicians get the prime seats inside the tiny bar while most of the audience sit at modest tables and chairs out on the patio. Always dance if you feel so moved, but be careful about chatting – customers guilty of speaking too loudly during a song will be met with a frown and a "shush!" from Alfredo.

zona norte

cascadura, méier,
praça da bandeira, tijuca

For most visitors to Rio (and many of the
city's wealthier locals, for that matter), the map of
Zona Norte might as well say "here be dragons". In size,
this sprawling area, made up of several neighborhoods,
dwarfs Zona Sul, and although points of interest are
sprinkled more thinly, there are still plenty of reasons
to venture north: Cascadura is home to some of Rio's
most famous samba schools; Tijuca boasts award-
winning bars; and Praça da Bandeira is becoming a
gastronomical oasis. The low rents and lack of dollar-
laden tourists mean that Zona Norte prices are far less
wince-inducing, and entrepreneurs are willing to take
more risks, whether that involves staying completely
faithful to old-school roots, or trying more experimental
business models, the one thing you won't find here is
middle-of-the-road tourist fodder.

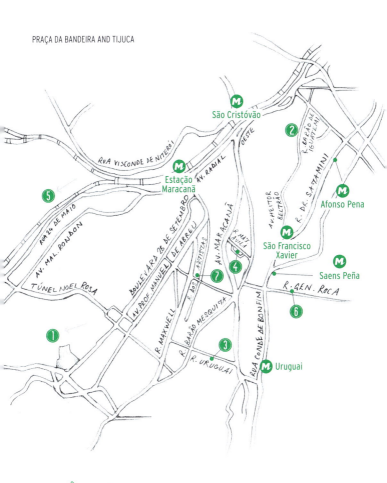

1 Barbearia do Zé (off map)
2 Bar da Frente
3 Bar do Momo
4 Casa Amarela
5 Gomes Calçados (off map)
6 Homegrown
7 Yeasteria

BARBEARIA DO ZÉ

Barber shop for the modern man

Rua Dias da Cruz, 170 (near Travessa Miracema) / **+55 21 3518 1859**
barbeariadoze.com.br / **Closed Monday**

Getting your hair cut in a place where you don't speak the language
can be pretty nerve-racking. Although I've never had any major disasters,
I found most hairdressers only offered a very basic service – a quick trim
and you'd be out on the street in 20 minutes. I was delighted to discover
Barbearia do Zé (aka male-grooming heaven) near the Méier train station.
In addition to a row of retro barber chairs, there's also a bar selling a
curated selection of artisanal beers. The interior is extremely stylish –
a mix of exposed brickwork, mirrors and moody lighting – giving this
the feel of an exclusive men's club from the 1930s. If having a beer and
getting your hair cut isn't enough, you can add a hot towel shave, have
your beard styled or your eyebrows shaped.

BAR DA FRENTE

Craft beers and inventive pub food

Rua Barão de Iguatemi, 388 (near Rua Felisberto de Menezes)
+55 21 2502 0176 / bardafrente.com.br / Closed Monday

The cheekily named Bar da Frente, meaning "the bar in front", sits in front of well-known Praça da Bandeira restaurant Aconchego Carioca. Though the bar originally took overflow customers from its busy neighbor, over time, it's made a name for itself; no one considers it a backup choice these days. Run by mother-daughter duo Valéria and Mariana Rezende, the bar stocks both domestic and imported craft brews, and the bolinhos de feijoada (bean croquettes stuffed with shredded collard greens and bacon) are my essential order – plus, they pair well with the zingy caipirinha. The menu also features some really unusual bar food creations such as fondue de coxinhas, breaded chicken croquettes that you dip into cheese and white wine fondue.

BAR DO MOMO

Sophisticated burgers in unlikely surrounds

Rua General Espírito Santo Cardoso, 50A (near Ria Uruguai)
+55 21 2570 9389 / **facebook.com/bardomomotijuca** / **Closed Sunday**

This little bar in Tijuca is the kind of place you'd walk straight past if you didn't know better; it looks like any other hole-in-the-wall – a steel counter and cheap plastic furniture spread across a sidewalk. Bar do Momo is a place for those who are willing to look past the superficial, and is a top pick of people in the know. Behind it all is Chef Toninho, whose fat, housemade burgers come with flourishes like Campari-caramelized onions and smoked paprika mayonnaise that you'd expect to find in high-end hipster joints. While the lunches served are more humble affairs that usually involve rice, beans or fish, the burgers and the specialty of the house, bolinhos de arroz (crispy, cheesy rice croquettes) are served from 4–9:30pm. There's also another thing you wouldn't expect in a simple bar like this – an impressive list of craft beers.

CASA AMARELA

Tattoo studio, art space and women's fashion and accessories

Rua Babilônia, 18A (near Rua Benjamin Franklin) / +55 21 3189 6658
coletivoca.com.br / Closed Sunday

Much like Coletivo 183 (see pg 29) in Botafogo, Casa Amarela is
a collective of independent designers, artisans and artists sharing a
bright yellow, two-story house in Tijuca. The rooms of the house are split
between the occupants: a tattoo studio run by artist Fernando Oliveira,
who specializes in monochrome and pointillism; an art exhibition space;
a store that sells bags, accessories and a funky collection of women's
clothes; and an area for workshops, performances and events. Casa
Amarela hosts classes led by their tenants and other artists, and also
occasional open-houses that usually involve food and live music – check
their Facebook page for updates on what's happening when.

GOMES CALÇADOS

Fancy shoes made to measure

Avenida Dom Hélder Câmara, 10506 (near Rua Silva Gomes)
+55 21 3273 0618 / facebook.com/Gomes-Calçados / Closed Sunday

Although the conventional stereotype of someone shoe-obsessed is female, there's a place for men to get in on the action here in Rio. For more than 50 years, Gomes Calçados has been making bespoke footwear for men. Many of the designs feature stripes, polka dots and other flamboyant touches, and are made in vividly colored leather. The vibrant designs are traditionally used by samba dancers during Carnival, but also work well for special occasions. It's far out in the neighborhood of Cascadura, a 45-minute drive from Centro, but with most pairs costing less than R$400 (around US$100), this is affordable luxury that is worth the taxi fare. Considering today's world of mass production, who can say they've had shoes tailored to fit their feet?

HOMEGROWN

A home for street art, urban fashion and more

Rua General Roca, 514 (near Praça Gustavo Capanema)
+55 21 3189 6661 / homegrown.com.br / Closed Sunday

In recent years, Rio's urban art scene has exploded, and this is reflected by a surge in gallery exhibitions, favela painting projects and educational workshops about street art. The Homegrown brand stands at the forefront of this movement – their first outlet in Ipanema is pretty compact, but the Tijuca store has a lot more space, allowing it to act as a multifunctional hub for various activities and events. There is an art gallery displaying works from some of the city's biggest names in urban art such as João Lelo, Bruno Big and Marcel Ment; a store stocking all the essential urban fashion accessories (T-shirts, sneakers, baseball caps, etc); plus a café, a bar and even a barber shop.

YEASTERIA

Brazilian craft brews

Rua Pereira Nunes, 266 (near Rua dos Artistas) / +55 21 3579 3003 yeasteria.com.br / Closed Sunday and Monday

I've always found Rio's beer scene interesting. Most places stock cheap, mass-produced, near-flavorless bottles of Skol and Brahma ("beer soda" as my wife calls them), and yet I've met more beer enthusiasts in this city than anywhere else. Turns out, the microbrewery scene here is booming, and if you know where to look, there are bars that serve artisanal creations. Yeasteria is top of the pile – the space is dominated by a huge set of shelves displaying 350 different bottles, about 200 of which are Brazilian (try the Three Monkeys golden ale or anything from Jeffrey Beer – both local breweries), and there are always three beers on tap as well as a small assortment of tasty bar snacks (mostly croquettes). If you're feeling overwhelmed, the manager, Merlin (his real name), speaks fluent English and will happily make recommendations according to your taste or area of interest.

lapa and centro

Rio's historical past mingles effortlessly with its future in the neighborhoods of Lapa and Centro. As evidenced by the towering glass office buildings separated by wide streets, Centro is the business hub. Sprinkled among the contemporary constructions are delightful older areas such as Saara shopping district and the Port Zone, home to the samba-centric neighborhood of Saúde as well as the revitalized Praça Mauá, which, thanks to the Olympics, now has a new public square featuring the gleaming Museum of Tomorrow. In contrast to Centro, Lapa really comes alive on weekends. The massive, white arches of the Carioca Aqueduct link Lapa to nearby Santa Teresa and also mark the area with the highest concentration of bars and live music venues in the city. Wandering down Avenida Mem de Sá, you'll pass lovely, stalwart restaurants, rowdy music venues and samba clubs that keep the neighborhood hopping until the wee hours of the morning.

1 Casa Paladino
2 Casa Turuna
3 Charutaria Syria
4 Confeitaria Colombo
5 Curto Café
6 Galeto 183
7 Granado Pharmacias
8 L'Atelier du Cuisinier
9 Mercado Moderno
10 Nova Capela Restaurante
11 Restaurante Albamar (off map)
12 Tropicália Discos

CASA PALADINO

Throwback bar and diner

Rua Uruguaiana, 224 (at Avenida Marechal Floriano)
+55 21 2263 2094 / No website / Open daily

Established in 1906, Casa Paladino is a bar and lunch venue that shows its age in the best possible way. Through the wide doors, you'll see huge glass-fronted shelves stacked to the ceiling with bottles of booze, and wood panels blackened with age that are plastered with hand-scrawled prices. In addition to the various cold cuts and drinks listed on the walls, there's also a menu listing dozens of regular Portuguese dishes, but the two stand-out specialties of the house are the triplo, a fat sandwich made with crusty bread and filled with ham, cheese and scrambled egg, and the omelet de bacalhau, a thick omelet made with generous quantities of salted cod. Heads up, they don't accept any credit or debit cards — truly old-school.

CASA TURUNA

Brazilian fabrics and Carnival costumes

Avenida Passos, 125 (near Rua Senhor dos Passos)
+55 21 2509 3908 / No website / Closed Sunday

Once Christmas is out of the way, Carnival lovers start their quest for a fantasia (costume). Most years, my get-up hunt starts and finishes at Casa Turuna, a textile and costume shop that celebrated its centenary in 2015. The space houses vast rolls of vivid fabrics, curly wigs, flamboyantly colored feather boas, streamers, glitter paint and tons of outfits for all ages, shapes and sizes. The store is busiest from the start of January until Carnival, which is in February or early March, but is open year-round. It's a phenomenal starting point for an exploration of Centro's Saara shopping district, a rabbit warren of miscellaneous shops centered around Rua da Alfândega and Rua Senhor dos Passos. Make sure to visit during the day, as the area can be deserted at night.

CHARUTARIA SYRIA

Cigar shop and café

Rua Senhor dos Passos, 180 (near Rua Regente Feijó)
+55 21 2224 9550 / No website / Closed Sunday

People are often surprised to learn that Brazil has a sizeable Arab population. In Rio, many of these Arab Brazilians settled in the area around Saara, and blessed the city with businesses like Charutaria Syria, opened in 1912 by a Syrian immigrant. "Charutaria" is the Portuguese word for a cigar shop, and although this store does sell some tobacco and smoking paraphernalia (note, however, there is no smoking permitted inside), I visit this place for its wonderful espresso, confections (try the chocolate-covered carrot cake) and general old-world charm. Walking into the narrow shop feels like stepping back in time – glass-fronted cabinets line the walls, displaying bottles of wine and pipes; there's also a 90-year-old advert painted directly onto the wall promoting a long-dead brand of matches. Around Carnival time, the streets of Saara can become extremely busy with shoppers hurrying to get their costumes – this is a magnificent place to have a time-out and rest your tired feet.

CONFEITARIA COLOMBO

Grand establishment serving French and Portuguese pastries

Rua Gonçalves Dias, 32 (near Rua 7 de Setembro) / +55 21 2505 1500
confeitariacolombo.com.br / Closed Sunday

Confeitaria Colombo has one of the most stately interiors of any building
in the city. Opened in 1894, this two-story, 200-seat café-and-restaurant
is a splendid example of Belle Époque design. With patterned tile floors,
huge mirrors and a massive stained-glass skylight, you will feel like
you've been transported to a majestic Parisian dining hall. Aside from
the ostentatious décor, it has a superb array of French and Portuguese
pastries such as mille-feuille (vanilla slice) and pastel de nata (Portuguese
egg tart) – combine with an espresso for the perfect morning pick-me-up
before touring nearby shops such as Granado Pharmácias (see pg 120) and
Tropicália Discos (see pg 125).

CURTO CAFÉ

Excellent pay-what-you-wish coffee

2nd Floor Edifício Garagem Menezes Côrtes, Avenida Erasmos Braga, 278 (near Avenida Presidente Antônio Carlos) / +55 21 98255 7424 facebook.com/curtocafe / Closed Saturday and Sunday

Located in a rather unglamorous Centro shopping mall, the first thing you'll notice at this remarkable café is the blackboard with figures that break down the business's monthly spending – from how much they paid for coffee beans to their accountant's fee. This is displayed to help you decide how much to pay for your drink. That's right; you pay what you like. What's more, the java is the tastiest in Rio. Don't expect the usual plethora of lattes and flat whites – they only have two options: espresso and cappuccino, brewed from beans (available to purchase whole or ground) sourced from independent farms in the neighboring state of Espírito Santo.

GALETO 183

Vintage recipes and local comforts

Rua Santana, 183 (near Rua Irineu Marinho) / +55 21 2252 3914
facebook.com/galeto183 / Closed Sunday

I'm always impressed when I meet someone who knows about Galeto 183. It's a modest-looking boteco (bar-restaurant) that rarely makes it onto most people's radar. Owner Ana Campos manages front of house, and will usher you to one of the tightly packed tables. Their special every Wednesday is the iconic local street food, angu do gomes (creamy polenta topped with a rich meaty stew). The handwritten recipe, given to Ana many years ago by its inventor, João Gomes, hangs framed on the wall. On other days, the must-order is a monster filet mignon that is large enough to share, served with rice, beans and tasty egg farofa. Regardless of when you go, always start with a basket of the scrumptious garlic bread and a limãozinho, a potent shot of cachaça, lime juice and sugar.

GRANADO PHARMACIAS

Emperor-approved grooming products

Rua Primeiro de Março, 16 (near Rua do Ouvidor) / **+55 21 3231 6746**
en.granado.com.br / **Closed Sunday**

When I have guests who are more into culture than beaches, I always steer them toward Centro — it's where Rio keeps its most interesting history. Case in point: nearly 150 years after this pharmacy was lauded by Brazil's Emperor Dom Pedro, the original Centro store is still going strong. Though I'm no emperor, I'll throw my endorsement in the mix as well since their vegetable glycerin soaps are integral to my grooming routine. The light, spacious shop has massive wooden dressers lining the walls topped with dizzying displays of soaps, shampoos, moisturizers, and other products for men and women. Much of their stock is made with local ingredients and extracts such as açaí and murumuru butter, and come with beautifully designed packaging that make their items smashing gifts.

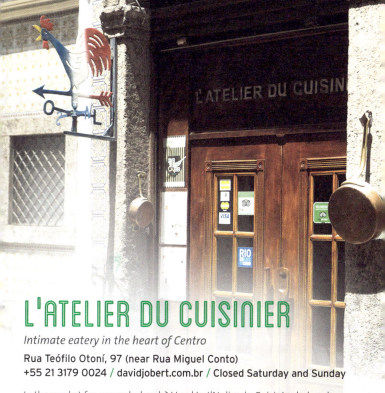

L'ATELIER DU CUISINIER

Intimate eatery in the heart of Centro

Rua Teófilo Otoní, 97 (near Rua Miguel Conto)
+55 21 3179 0024 / davidjobert.com.br / **Closed Saturday and Sunday**

In the market for a swanky lunch? Head to L'Atelier du Cuisinier, helmed by Chef David Jobert, who, after proving himself at three-Michelin-starred Auberge de l'ill in France and La Cigale hotel in Qatar, moved to Rio, opened this delightful bistro in 2012 and decided to do things his own way: the restaurant only opens for lunch and seats 26 people. Although the space is compact, it doesn't feel cramped, and the décor of art and racks of copper pans lend a pleasingly traditional atmosphere. The modern French menu is small – just two or three options each for entrée, main and dessert – and while the prices aren't low, I've always felt that the three-course executive menu offers great value, and it includes a divine crème brûlée.

MERCADO MODERNO

Retro Brazilian furniture and design gallery

Rua do Lavradio, 130 (near Rua do Rezende) / +55 21 2508 6083
mercadomodernobrasil.com.br / Closed Sunday

Linking Lapa and Centro, Rua do Lavradio is packed with remarkable old buildings adorned with intricate wrought-iron balconies. In such a historical area, it seems fitting that many of these somewhat crumbling structures are home to stores selling antiques and curios. While many of the shops on this street have no name and stock items that have seen better days, this one stands out as something special. Arranged within the lovingly restored room is an exquisite stock of chairs, tables, lamps, wardrobes and other design pieces dating from the 1950s to the 1980s. This is an upscale collection, so don't expect to pick up any low-value bargains, but the store works just as well as a viewing gallery.

NOVA CAPELA RESTAURANTE

Tried-and-true Portuguese-Brazilian food

Avenida Mem de Sá, 96 (near Rua do Lavradio) / **+55 21 2252 6228**
facebook.com/Nova-Capela-Restaurante / Open daily

Nova Capela is exactly the type of place you'd walk straight past if you didn't know any better. The outside is unremarkable – all you see is frosted glass windows and a small sign above the door. Once you walk in, you'll understand why this is a Lapa institution. The waiters, many of whom have worked here for more than 20 years, wear smart white jackets and clearly take much pride in their work. The specialties here are bolinhos de bacalhau (salted cod croquettes) and cabrito assado, which translates to roast goat, but they actually use lamb. The restaurant's Portuguese roots are seen in many other items as well as in the customary red, decorative tiles that line the walls. On weekends, the restaurant stays open until 4am, ideal as a late-night supper spot after catching some of Lapa's lively nightlife.

RESTAURANTE ALBAMAR

Seafood establishment steeped in history

Praça Marechal Âncora, 184 (near Avenida Alfred Agache)
+55 21 3228 8644 / albamar.com.br / Open daily

The story of Restaurante Albamar's building is so interesting that if it wasn't a restaurant I expect it would be a museum. It began in 1908, when glass was imported from Antwerp to construct four octagonal towers of a huge municipal market situated right on Guanabara Bay, a stone's throw from Praça XV. Sadly, the market and three of its towers were demolished in the 1960s. The lone tower that survived now houses this high-end yet pleasingly retro seafood restaurant. Don't expect culinary trends like obscurely flavored foams or 15-course tasting menus — instead, the chef concentrates on timeless French and Italian preparations of seafood, including the freshest oysters and some unusual Amazonian fish such as pirarucu and tambaqui. The waterside location, coupled with panoramic views, make this a top choice for a special occasion.

TROPICÁLIA DISCOS

A vinyl treasure trove

Praça Olávo Bilac, 28, Store 207 (near Rua do Rosário)
+55 21 2224 9215 / facebook.com/tropicalia.discos
Closed Saturday and Sunday

The first piece of music I ever bought was a seven-inch vinyl single (Paul Hardcastle's "19" since you ask), and even though digital is all the rage now, it's hard to beat the old-school music format. If your ideal afternoon is flipping through old 12-inch albums, then Tropicália Discos is an essential stop. Owners Márcio Rocha and Bruno Alonso stock more than 30,000 records, and have no prejudice when it comes to music – you'll find Brazilian essentials: samba, bossa nova and MPB (popular Brazilian music) as well as international music including rock, jazz, blues, reggae and classical. If there's something you like, the staff will stick it on the turntable for you to have a listen before you commit.

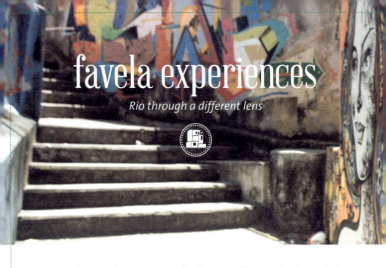

favela experiences

Rio through a different lens

A symbol of Rio's massive urbanization, more than 600 favelas – which translates to slums – can be found throughout the city. While they have a bit of a reputation (for good reason), they can be spirited, interesting communities, and it's become common for visitors to take tours, visit bars, hike trails and stay in hostels located in such places. Although crime hasn't been entirely eradicated, the safety of many favelas has improved significantly since Pacifying Police Units (UPP) were introduced in 2008. If you're in any doubt about navigating one, hire a reputable, local guide (most hotels can provide a list of recommendations), or try one of the following for an enriching experience.

American-Brazilian Zezinho is a proud resident of Rocinha, the city's largest favela, which is located between São Conrado and Gávea. On **Zezinho's Tour**, you'll explore the area, meet the residents and gain an understanding of how the favela operates. The tour proceeds go toward the Spin Rocinha DJ School, which teaches young kids to DJ, and also support local bars and restaurants.

Towering above the Vidigal favela, which overlooks Ipanema Beach, are the twin peaks of Dois Irmãos. The starting point of the trail for the one-hour **Dois Irmãos Trek** is located at the very top of the community and can be safely

CAMINHO DO GRAFITE
Rua Almirante Alexandrino 3286 (near Rua Gomes
Lopes), no phone, facebook.com/SantaPrazeresTour

DOIS IRMÃOS TREK
Trail begins: Vila Olímpica do Vidigal, no phone
etrilhas.com.br, open daily

PROJETO MORRINHO TOUR
Rua Pereira da Silva, 826 (near Rua Engenheiro
Alfredo Modrach), +55 21 98308 6298
projetopereirao.wordpress.com

ZEZINHO'S TOUR
Meeting point: Posto 9 (near Avenida Pedro Moura)
+55 21 98221 5572, favelatour.org

followed independently or with a guide. The views from the top are breathtaking:
a terrific payoff for the hard work put in to hike up.

The **Projeto Morrinho Tour** takes you into the Pereira da Silva favela, near
Santa Teresa, to view the eponymous installation. Made from cinder blocks,
the colorful, 350 sq m (around 3,800 sq ft) model of a favela is incredibly
detailed: it includes lights, cable-cars, stores, roads and vehicles, as well as
scenes from daily life. The project provides employment for a dozen people
who maintain the model and guide tours. Note: visits to the project must
be arranged in advance.

Rio's favelas have long been hotbeds of creativity, so it's fitting that the
Caminho do Grafite, which translates to "graffiti path", is located in a favela
near Santa Teresa. This path is 100 m (330 ft) and features vivid artworks from
45 artists. Tours are guided by young residents of the Santa Prazeres favela and
can be set up through their Facebook page.

Travel the World with The HUNT Guides

The HUNT: Global Cities Boxed Set

Hong Kong | London | New York City | Paris | San Francisco

The HUNT: U.S. Cities Boxed Set

Austin | Boston | New Orleans | New York City | San Francisco